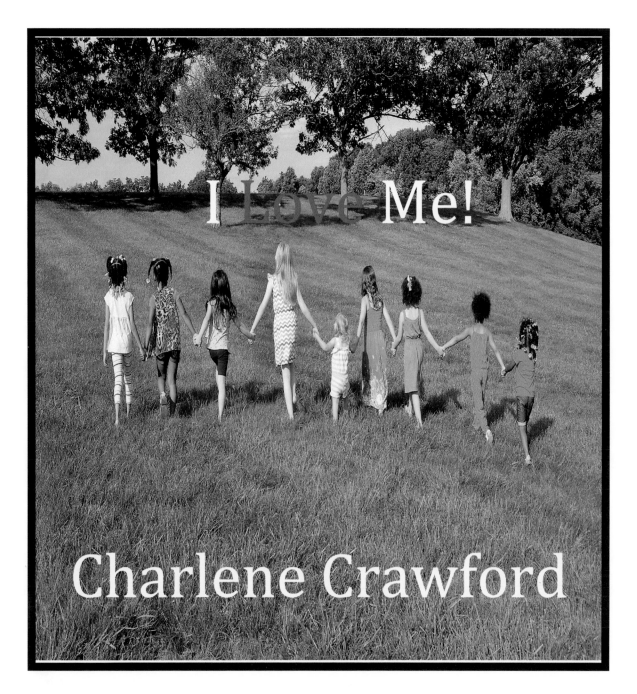

I Love Me!

Charlene Crawford

Copyright 2015

I Love Me

By Charlene Crawford
Photographs by Charlene Crawford, Ana Crawford, and Rick
Stylist Anissa Robinson and Ana Crawford
Editor: Arlene Thomas
Contributor: George Hart

Printed in the United States of America

ISBN 978-0-9794033-9-2

Library of Congress Cataloging-in-Publication Data
Library of Congress Control Number: 2015911718

Crawford, Charlene E. 1972-
I Love Me/ Charlene Crawford

Summary: I love me is a picture book of self-esteem. The book encourages children to love their body just the way it is and encourages them to accept and appreciate the differences in others.
To receive curriculum to use with the book visit the author's website@
www.charlenecrawford.com

I Love Me!

Charlene Crawford

Sight Words:

I

like

love

me

my

we

I like my hair.

We love our hair.

We love our hair.

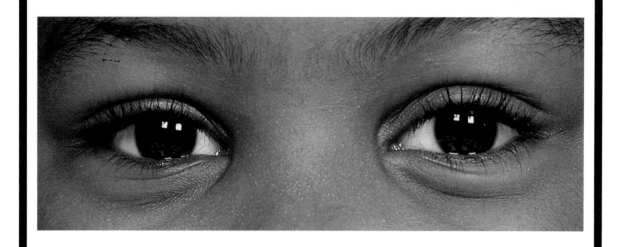

I like my eyes.

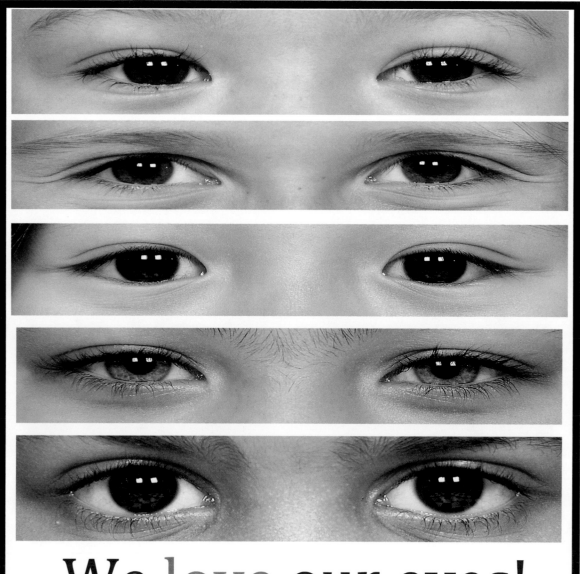

We love our eyes!

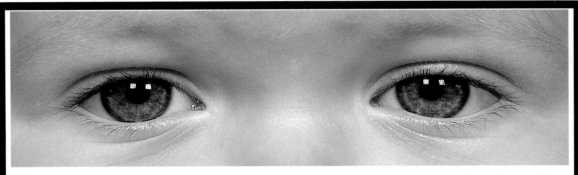

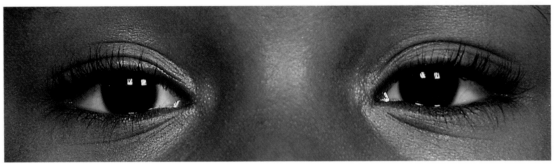

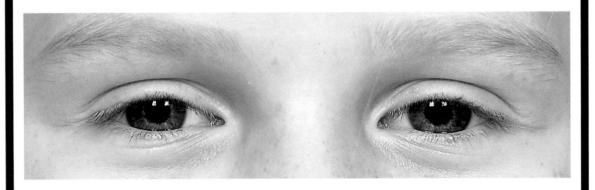

We love our eyes!

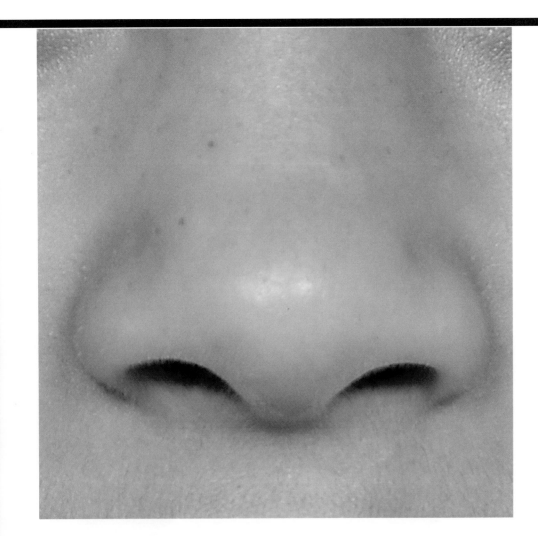

I like my nose.

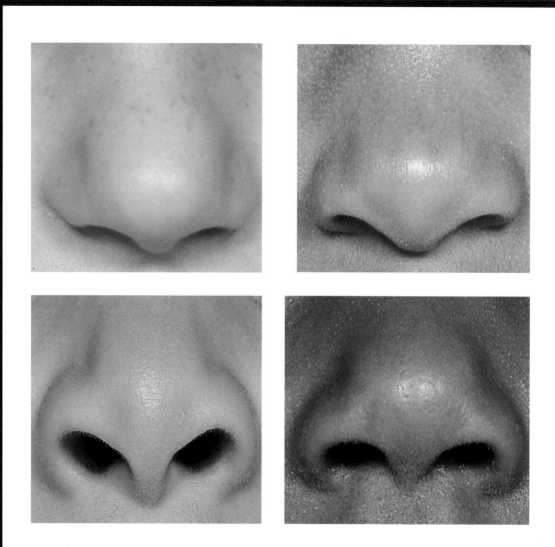

We love our noses!

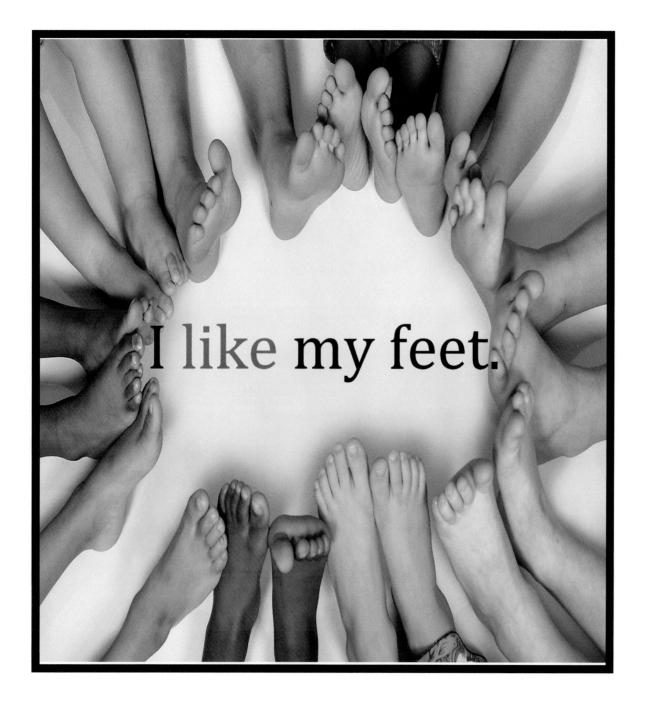

We love our feet.

I like my hands.

We love our hands!

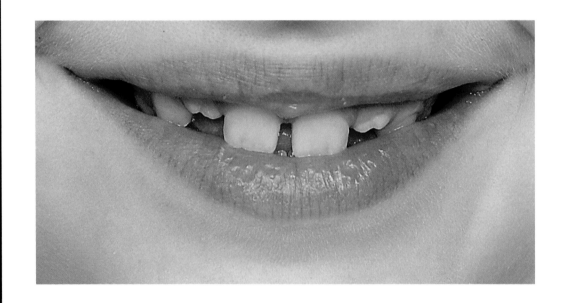

I like my smile.

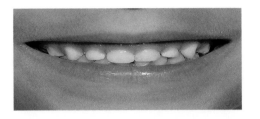
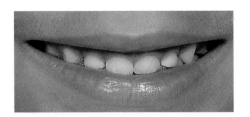
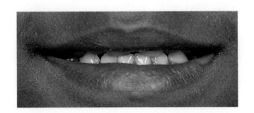

We love our smiles!

I love me just the way I am!

We love each other just the way we are.

Visit www.charlenecrawford.com to download the preschool/primary anti-bullying curriculum free for a limited time.
(SAMPLE LESSON)

POSITIVE CONFESSION:
I AM BEAUTIFULLY AND WONDERFULLY MADE.

Leader: Did you see any pictures of hair in the book? Allow the child(ren) to look through the pictures. They will be excited to show you what they found.

Leader: What do we have on top of our head?

Child response: varies (guide them to answer hair)

Leader: What does the hair on your head do?

Child response: Varies (guide them or suggest that it helps to keep the skin on our head from sun burn, it helps the body stay warm.)

Leader: What if you don't have hair?

Child response: Varies (guide them that they could use a hat, sunscreen, or scarf.)

Leader: Having or not having hair doesn't matter. The color or if it is long or short, curly or straight, just remember you are beautiful. You were fearfully and wonderfully made.

Leader: Please repeat after me. "I am beautifully"

Child: "I am beautifully"

Leader: "and wonderfully "

Child: "and wonderfully "

Leader: "made!"

Child: "made!"

(Please repeat 2 additional times building excitement in your voice for the final turn. If the child can handle larger phrases, please feel free to use it.)

Charlene Crawford, a certified teacher and former Director of Christian Education for HVPC, has worked with children and literature for almost 30 years. She has earned her Bachelor's degree in Education from Temple University, her Master's degree from Arcadia University in computers and technology in the classroom, administration and leadership and also her principal and ESOL certification. She was the owner of Crawford Education Plus, a successful tutoring program for 20 years. Charlene Crawford was inducted into the National Association of Professional Women and the Cambridge Who's Who for all of her accomplishments: Charlene was the 1998 Outstanding Educator recipient. Crawford was the recipient of the 2007 Editors Choice Award for her poem African Woman of God. She is also a published international poet and her first published book, Adventures with Granny in the Garden, was nominated Best Children's Christian Book of the year.

This former talk show host for "Living Abundantly," Camp Director, and Appointed Reading Specialist for the Philadelphia I.Y.W.C.C. YET program finds her greatest joy sharing the word of God, writing children's stories, helping others, and spending time with her husband, children, and family.